2011

Every Dress a Decision

Every Dress a Decision

Elizabeth Austen

Blue Begonia Press   Selah, Washington

Cover art: Peggy Bacon in mid-air backflip, Bondi Beach,
Sydney, Feb. 6, 1937. By Ted Hood.
Author photograph: Fat Yeti Photography
Cover design by Amy Peters.

Library of Congress Cataloging-in-Publication Data

Austen, Elizabeth.
 Every dress a decision / Elizabeth Austen.
    p. cm.
 ISBN 978-0-911287-64-6 (alk. paper)
 I. Title.
 PS3601.U854E94 2011
 811'.6--dc22

                              2011008541

Blue Begonia Press
311 Hillcrest Drive   Selah, WA 98942
bluebegoniapress.com

for Eric

and in memory of my brother
Michael Hobbs
June 4, 1960 – June 21, 1997

The Spirit lurks within the Flesh
Like Tides within the Sea
That make the Water live, estranged
What would the Either be?

—Emily Dickinson

A brother never ends. I prowl him. He does not end.

—Anne Carson

We can do without pleasure,
but not delight.

—Jack Gilbert

Contents

One

Two

THREE

ONE

House Fire

I reach for my yellow dress. It bursts
into flame. Anything I remember
burns again. Recipes from Nana's walnut box,
father's letters, every photograph: all
the same black exhalation—
the remains of everything consumed
coat the remains of everything spared.
Memories reduced to images without
objects to anchor them hover
in the space between this morning—
when each room stood intact—
and now, a time without geography.
Nothing ties me to the past.
No family portraits, no letters
urging goodness, steadiness, obedience.
All the old imperatives
curl in the lingering heat.

It Didn't Happen That Way

Unless the apple itself, longing
to be known, can be blamed
for the light bent
across its skin,
for the midday heat
transforming sugar to scent.

And him? She didn't say
a word to him. He found her
slack-jawed,
skin flushed and damp
as if he had lain on her,
pressed into her—

he found her, swallow by swallow
savoring the taste of knowledge,
her eyes fixed, focused

somewhere beyond him
as if he no longer existed.
And one more thing—
she didn't tempt him. In fact
she never offered it.

He pried the fruit
from her hand, desperate
to follow, and bit.

WHAT IS KNOWN

for my brother Michael

the office   my desk   phone
ringing   our mother's voice   the news
the office   my desk   phone ringing
our mother's voice
the news in my hand   the office desk
phone ringing   mother's voice in my hand
her voice in my hand ringing
our mother   her voice   the news
ringing   ringing

Problem Was

Problem was, we lived in a house the size of a subway car
and the problem was it wasn't just us in there but a dog
bred for long runs on the Alaskan tundra and he—
the man, my boyfriend—he'd need to fight, to lay it out,
all the real ways—I see that now—I'd disappointed him—
day after day he'd save it up until evening—
it was always evening in that house—come evening
he'd let it spill—
all the evidence of my selfishness, immaturity, laziness—
the way I never remembered to fill the tank
when I borrowed his car, or which shirts
went in the dryer—and looking back from here
I see how right he was, how small and closed-fisted
the love I had to offer really was, how inadequate
to his need. We fought over all the normal things—
where the money went, sex—always too little, ill-timed or
incomplete—who was to blame for that, for letting
the dog out. Of course it didn't help that we'd wait until dark
to get down to it, finally worn down beyond the leash
of politeness, each of us a fine, steady abrasion
against the other. How could we help it? He hated
how I drew the tiny brush of liquid lacquer
across each fingernail and I hated how,
when traffic in our small city clotted and snarled, how it
unnerved him—when he wanted me to dress like the hippie girl
I'd appeared at first to be and did not yet—
you understand—recognize even myself that I was not—
when we fought, he would raise his voice, nothing inappropriate,
no threat of violence, but the problem was
as soon as the simmering tension broke into outright conflict
my blood would slow, heart rate easing back, breath shallow,
the weight of my eyelids insupportable. The more he talked—
his litany of needs, the catalog of my flaws, the chronicle

of his disappointments—it became a kind of lullaby, soporific,
setting me adrift on the tundra, swooning into a stupor—
sweet sleep cocooning me from every obvious, persistent clue.
We were doomed. Livid, he'd shake me awake and sure enough
I'd deny sleeping. I didn't believe him. Who falls asleep
in the middle of an argument? So muddled—you understand—
so foreign, even to myself.

My Uterus, That Party Balloon

never inflated

dancehall
with a no-show
band

shoebox full
of tissue

invitation
unaddressed

vacant buffet

SCENE: HOTEL, INTERIOR

he holds over his head   her dress
vacant and anonymous   her body
folds   her mind   a curtain dropping

the soundtrack next door
porn's percussive
dialogue   laughter

the dress a banner over his head
a blank flag   a page he turns
from a script her body won't recite

a houseful of locks
clicks shut   her refusal
a body between them

she takes the dress from his hand
fills the dress with her decision
wraps her arms over her clothed breasts

he empties his eyes   the dress
a mistranslated subtitle   a trailer
with no feature

he offers one foot to each pant leg
accepts the sigh of his zipper   a clock
gathers their silence

WHAT IS KNOWN

for weeks before   I heard it   saw it
the premonition   again and again—
office   desk   phone   voice
news   it happened
exactly as I saw it
only one detail wrong—
you   how could it be you

Good-bye, My Millions

*At twenty weeks' gestation, the peak of a female's
oogonial load, the fetus holds 6 to 7 million eggs.*
—Natalie Angier, Woman*

The husband will proffer but here's what he
offers: denatured, defused—a deliberate
blank. You cast in vain your thread of welcome
little debutante, pod of potential
(packet of proteins and chromosomes).
You play to an empty house
on a darkened stage. No more
unto the breach, no more. Your gentleman
caller's all shine, no spark. His wallet holds
nothing but counterfeit notes. I know
you can't help it—your nature to ripen
and leap, linger by the phone for the call.
Invisible. Not viable. Again, as always,
this scene must end in blood.

Defusing the Time Bomb

*...the population clock keeps ticking, with a net
of 2.5 more mouths to feed born every second*
—Joel K. Bourne, Jr., "The End of Plenty"
National Geographic

When they offer the sedative, accept.
Your partner may sit beside you. Relax
as the doctor administers local.
Relax!

Relax while he makes a small puncture.
This method's success rate is high:
Separate vas from sheath. Cut and seal
with electrocautery.

Cautery is temporary, but
will stimulate a strong scar. Repeat
other side. After a few minutes
dress and leave. No stitches needed.

The small opening
will seal itself.

Only Say the Word and I Shall Be Healed

I started a dinnertime rhyming game
muck nuck luck duck huck fuck—
and learned the power of a word
from the looks on their faces. Each night
we hail-mary-ed and our-father-ed
away the day's bruises—me and God
getting Mom's undivided attention for all
ninety-seven words. I watched the priest
raise Christ. His words, the rhythm, my knees
wobbling—I fainted right there on the altar.
Mother said it was that I hadn't eaten breakfast but
I knew the power of those words. And if
mass had still been in Latin, who knows? I
might have ignited right there from the sheer
brilliance of the syllables. But I was
born too late for that kind of miracle.

LEAVING THE ISLAND

ferry from Orcas to Anacortes

Mist-colored knots of sea glass. A moss-clot
cadged from the trail's edge. The truce

fished word by word from beneath the surface,
still unspoken. We carry what we found

what we made there. Three days you and I
let the currents direct our course, slept

on cool sand, let woodsmoke flavor us.
What's left? Slow travel over cold water.

Toward home and days ordered by clocks
instead of tides. We watch through salt-scarred

windows, hoping the dark shapes will rise
beside us, will grace us. We know too well

what can't be willed, only missed
if we look away too soon.

Between Floors

Another solo shopper and I step into the car, past
a boy peering out, *Mom?* The doors shut. To no one

in particular, *I need 5.* Solo shoppers look away.
The boy no more than 6. Not yet panicking.

We rise, doors open, he turns, no hesitation
looks me full in the face. Is it because I stand nearest?

Not this floor, not yet. He is satisfied with my answer.
The door clicks shut. We rise.

Does he believe all grown-up women
are somebody's mommy?

Doors open. More shoppers fill the car. Packed together,
it is me his eyes ask, my word he takes. *Next one.*

How long will he keep this illusion
of a world conspiring to see him safely home?

A shrill bell, the doors slide apart. *There you are!*
He's out, no backward glance. I exhale a small prayer of thanks

for the free gift of his trust, for him seeing the possible mother
still alive in my face.

SCENE: INTERIOR, NIGHT

one thin wall a narrow world away
he sleeps I pace
morning a narrow hall
one thin wall worlds away
he sleeps I pace one room
between us sleeps a world
away I pace one wall
a narrow bed a world
pole to pole I pace
he sleeps he dreams
a world away

For Lost Sainthood

because when the Virgin
appeared She said nothing

just waved   less *hello* than
come this way

a third-grade girl   a faith-fevered
girl   I pledged my unknown

ungovernable body
consecrated my virginity to Hers

but already I knew
I burned

before knowledge before
even the barest mechanics

before the trancelike tidal pull
of sweat and flesh

I burned I burned
and already

I knew
I was not good   for all my hot

true tears when the host
was raised as Jesus' flesh

for all my prayers and carefully
counted rosary beads I knew

I burned I burned

FALSE SPRING

Frost, again, brittles the grass,
darkens the reckless bud.

Our breaths: a kind of weather
we make between us, partly cloudy.
We skirt the pond's icy cap—

eyeing the single glove, its handless
caress, frozen against a branch.

Consequence

In case the river calls me, I carry
two stones. But this is a lie, Virginia.
I have only enough courage to carry on.
These stones are nothing more
than pocketed threats. I am not
anyone I expected to be.
Give me some message, dreamer,
or give me back my sleep. Are we here
by grace? Virginia, you knew
the consequences of silence.
This page is the only prayer I know, the line
I follow into darkness. Is there anything
the body, the breakable body
can say or save?

BROTHER

eleven years old   a curious boy
a little sister nearby   willing

to do whatever you asked
I was six   what did I know

except   for a few indelible moments

my body   the absolute center
of my big brother's attention

it was as simple as that

years later I thought I understood
what had fractured that afternoon

I wrote   *you did*
this damage   you wrote

I'm sorry   can we
be OK   words on a page

you wanted it to be
as simple as that

I fold and unfold your letters
your obituaries

useless   these lopsided conversations
no reason not to trust you now

I am not that girl
and you are not

anything   who am I
to forgive   now that I always

have the last
useless word

HUMANS

a brief and strange species
—W. S. Merwin

the day begins in disarray *you ought you should you must*
you must you must you must   the bees will not

be stilled   what stitches mind to body   who cues the unraveling
if it's true we're infused with something not found in doorknob bird or bee

why am I confused about all the important things   crows
trampoline the power lines from house to house   they don't care

who runs the world   I gape at the sky   color of sunflower
color of blood   the world is not as I have believed it to be

I find no vantage   no long view across even the surface
peristalsis propels the worm into darkness   electricity

animates the lamp   the leaf drinks at the top of the tree
I understand none of the beautiful things   the sparrow bathes

in dirt   I don't know why   the birds do not ask themselves
or each other how are we to live   they do not ask us to love them

TWO

The Permanent Fragility of Meaning

Why persist, scratching across the white field
row after row? Why repeat the ritual
every morning, emptying my hands
asking for a new prayer to fold
and unfold?

                Nothing changes, no one is saved.

I walk into the day, hands still
empty and beg
to be of use to someone. I lie down
in the dark and beg to believe
when the voice comes again with its commands,
its promises—
                Unfold your hands. Revelation
is not a fruit you pluck from trees. This is the work,
cultivating the smallest shoot, readying your tongue
to shape the sacred names, your mouth already filling—

I lie down in the dark.

I rise up and begin again.

IN THE BRIDES' HOUSE

We know nuns' bodies do not function like ours.
Sister Carlotta blows her nose all day
and never exhausts the one tissue she keeps
tucked in the left cuff of her light blue cardigan.

What Is Known

the police report   translated from the Czech
tells us what we already know
you were found alone
in your bathtub   though the newspapers
speculate *vražda* or *sebevražda*   the coroner
can tell us nothing—
your body alone in water too long—
translation of cause no longer possible

GIRL WITH STONE IN HAND

You, girl of twenty-five. Here's a thing
to consider—he believes in the color

of your hair. You turn in sunlight
and he sees cave walls painted red-ochre

feels the heat of beach fires at night.
Your artifice carries weight

has implications. You, girl of twenty-five.
The stone you let fall

is still dropping—that wave
has yet to find its shore.

WHAT WE WOULD FORGET

ties us to the past
and   like roots beneath pavement   cracks

the surface we would pass across
though the tree lies some distance away

once heaved up and split
how can the path be smoothed

unless that living thing   *we must remember*
is uprooted

for *these things sometimes happen*   though
the details differ   ours is not a unique story

and if   as my lover enters me   my brother's
face intrudes   what am I to do

but open my eyes and name this man
who is not my brother   name myself   who am not

that girl   and continue the embrace
of these our bodies   now

no perception comes amiss
my senses learned their scope

in that child-body   *who was I then*
and what of that girl lives tonight

in my skin   do I carry her
always about me   ready to rise

and bind the present   this touch
to the past

WHAT IS KNOWN

the can of ashes   your name

ACCESSORY

> *When you're neutral, you're an accessory.*
> —Christiane Amanpour

I report on time   avert
my gaze   sing along
spend on cue   always
smell clean

I tie the slipknot   sharpen the knife
count out the pills   I load
the syringe   put ice in the glass
pour and pour and pour and pour

RECOMPOSE

why do I keep trying to talk to you
the dead don't care what we write

they've forgotten   even you
how to read   where you were   now

a question mark   an unresolved ellipsis
a stranger at the edge of my peripheral vision

do you see how hard I am trying to keep you
from vanishing   word by word

everything is still possible   I hear you tell me
only it's me telling me   wishing it was you

I know that   you don't have to remind me again
Dad in the hospital

all of us standing around his bed   useless
hands at our sides   your absence

crowding the air   *he would be here*   we think to ourselves
he would know what to do

Luxury

Intact, untapped—why say what goes unused
is wasted?

       Once I close my eyes
       I can't be trusted.

Not an accident or oversight.
A deliberate absence, scheduled vacancy.

       I birth a grain of rice every night,
       lose and find and lose all
       my small progeny. Who
       can hold a child no bigger
       than a grain of rice and the world
       so big around her?

I knew what I was saying no to.

       So who is it wakes me, whispering,
       We must give our lives
       to something, if not someone.

I pick up the story
where we last left off, turn the pages,
tuck blankets around borrowed daughters,
kiss each one goodnight.

       Some questions can't be answered
       with maybe.

FROM DR. SCHNARCH'S MARRIED PEOPLE'S SEX MANUAL

Orgasm: your brains fall out.
Having a neocortex is a liability
if you want to be a sex machine.

That's where the quantum model
can help. Friction plus fantasy.
Low-level anxiety is why sexual

novelty can be so enticing.
Normal marital sadism:
It turns vitriol

into lubrication. Where's
your head during sex? Couples
who don't play

with each other's genitals often
play with each other's
minds instead. When

was the last time
you felt that
with your partner?

ON PUNCTUATION

not for me the dogma of the period
preaching order and a sure conclusion
and no not for me the prissy
formality or tight-lipped fence
of the colon and as for the semi-
colon call it what it is
a period slumming
with the commas
a poser at the bar
feigning liberation with one hand
tightening the leash with the other
oh give me the headlong run-on
fragment dangling its feet
over the edge give me the sly
comma with its come-hither
wave teasing all the characters
on either side give me ellipsis
not just a gang of periods
a trail of possibilities
or give me the sweet interrupting dash
the running leaping joining dash all the voices
gleeing out over one another
oh if I must
punctuate
give me the YIPPEE
of the exclamation point
give me give me the curling
cupping curve mounting the period
with voluptuous uncertainty

SARAH

My nose on top of your head, I inhale
your version of the universal
baby scent, two parts vanilla, one part
wet earth. You rub your blanket across
your cheek, suckle the bottle. We've escaped
the throng of strange faces, too-loud voices.
One of us had a meltdown, overwhelmed
by everything we don't yet have words for.
Beyond that door, it's your mother's birthday.
She won't need us to explain what keeps us
from the party. Wrapped in the nursery's
familiar embrace, your body at ease
against mine, we rock.
The comforted, the comforter.

LILIES

They know they're spent.

Color blown out, scent disgorged,
they've begun to mutter among themselves.
They know they're my first, the only ones
to make it from bulb to blossom under my hand.

Now what?
I wear a trail from car door to front door
glancing sidelong at their browning bodies.
Mow them down? Let them dry up? They know I don't know.

Emptying their daylight bodies, they dismantle
the display. Each gathers the necessary
darkness, listens
for a wind, a wing—
with or without me, ready for the next life.

Prayer for Relief

Dear God
Please let me write a funny poem.
Seven days on the island and so far it's
death, death, death, death and
grief, which is to say, death.

Rabbits graze on the lawn but all I see
are hawk's talons sinking
into pale brown fur. Flies loiter
at the window pane
—death's backup singers.

It doesn't help, God, that I'm here
in autumn, poets' favorite
season. Trees turning skeletal,
cloudy nights dark as a grave, days
shortening like what remains of my life.

Dear God, this isn't remotely
funny. I wait at the window
steady as an undertaker
transcribing whatever you offer.
Promise me, at least

you'll give me the punch line
before I go.

Vestigial God, I.

Don't assume I believe in you
just because I'm talking to you.

✧

Actually, I'm between gods at the moment—

✧

saving my breath for someone who's not
too rude to do his own PR

✧

I can't go for a god who'd let himself be repped
by these spit-shineyspeedtalkingcashwavingflagcraving—

✧

I've been known to fall asleep at the wheel myself.

✧

I ask god to speak. I keep talking. What do I expect?

A MOMENT AGO

nothing happened
the couch still green   the month
still February   every chair

presses the carpet with the same
shape and force   nothing happened

we each wear
the same face   still
breathe   that tonnage

of kindling our voices
felled split peeled and stacked
a moment ago   nothing

happened   still
every floorboard

listens waits
for the match flare
not possible until—

Nobody's Mother

Only saints and the insane—and very small children—
don't care what others think of them.

૭

In Saudi Arabia, possession of ovaries—
functioning or not—disqualifies one for a driver's license.

૭

She who brings an empty dish to the feast is seldom invited
back again.

૭

Choice, the ultimate luxury.

૭

Every mother craves an understudy.

For You, First Through the Door

*...police say Hobbs was found dead last Thursday
and the cause of death was still unclear.*
—John Mastrini, *Prague Newsroom*

For the wall of stench
you clamber over.
For the futile handkerchief.

For your first body:
a bloated thing
barely human, for

you, first through his door
vomiting into the toilet
beside him, the air

purpling. For all you must
touch. For you, lying down
that night beside

your wife. For trying to sleep.
His taste still in your mouth.
Praise you.

EBBING HOUR

after Kunitz

Don't offer opiates.
Lay me naked in the ocean's
hammock, still awake enough
to know myself her own.
Feet on her salt pillow,
hands at last with nothing
to grasp. For once I'll
face unblunted
an event's full force.
I don't want to miss
the last important thing
I'll ever do. Let those
friends who remain
wade out with me
beyond the breakers and push.
I want to ride the swell.

THREE

How the End Begins

You ask what I think
and all the sparrows
abandon the tree.

You ask how I feel.
The ivy burns
up the side of the house.

You ask if I love you
and each line
erases itself from the map.

Shh. Isn't the shiver, the swing,
our bodies' thrill and flicker—
isn't that enough?

OVERHEAD, UNDERFOOT

Useless Bay, Whidbey Island

sandpipers clean the beach   one
flea at a time   the wrecked boat

bleached anonymous   herons
disperse like sentries along the tide line

tail without its rabbit   a fortune
in sand dollars   twice each day

the sea pretends to give back
what it takes   I walk from here to there

here to elsewhere   scraps float
across the marsh   *once was lost*

blind but now   are you hiding
or are you always on the move   a flock

of terns   scattering   gathering
shifting wordless on the wind

.

In Praise of Orality

an infant manifesto

only love the world wetly
lean in, lick the nearest anything,
bathe it in sweet spit, the delicious
suck of discovery

o mouth, omnivorous organ!
o edible kingdom!

soon, soon we meet by sight,
arm's length, in words—
leaving more and more
world untasted

HER, AT TWO

Sometimes a bone
at the tender back of the throat
requires a wracking, indelicate
cough to survive it. Sometimes
a bone is plucked

fully fleshed
from the platter and brandished
like a baton, a magician's wand.
She transfixes every guest,
gluttonous tyrant

in miniature. Is this how we all
began, thrilled to hold the meat
in our tiny fists, sure
the feast was laid for us
alone? Soon she will want

what she cannot reach,
will be told it's not for her
that's not ladylike,
wipe your fingers,
put down the bone.

Oh let her be lucky
and rare, let it be years
before her sex is learned
as limitation, a fence
to circumscribe her life.

Before that verdict is delivered
let her travel so far
into her own skin
she'll shrug off that suit

of expectations, clothe
her mind according to her own
desires, bite the flesh
from the bone. I want
to be her and want
to have birthed her

and I want her
to survive. That girl—
who reaches and takes, erupts
in glee as she shakes her fistful
of bone and meat.

Scene: Interior, Day

I have left the door ajar.
From the kitchen, the jangle
of pots and bowls, a cupboard
opened, then closed. You made

a vow to give me this kind of love—
my separate hours. Your footfall,
your underbreath conversation
with cookbook and knives, this

intermittent silence suspended,
elastic, between us. You open
a drawer, choose the tool for your task,
close the drawer as I turn the page.

A spoon clanks against a bowl, a pen
scratches against paper, "I have left
the door ajar…" A knock, your voice
through the crack. *Any lemons left?*

Limes. I listen to your steps
back to the kitchen.
The neighbors call to their kids
and the crows resume their clatter.

Now the task you set before me—
to shoulder my share
of blessings, make room
for every dish at the feast.

Vestigial God, II.

I miss the certainty. The visions.
Singing along.

⁊

Since we sexed you male.

⁊

My ex exoskeleton.

⁊

Too much carnage bears your fingerprints.

⁊

All right. That's fair—
there are those others. But why should you get the credit
for their goodness?

⁊

⁊

Still, it *will* rain
if we wait long enough.

What Is Known

a single fly   perhaps
pacing the windowsill

the last sound you registered—
perhaps—
a stirring of wings

WHERE CURRENTS MEET

Cattle Point, San Juan Island

See? Even at slack water a churn
of contradictions. Stay back, instinct

instructs. But from here, more beauty than danger.
Water is its own gravity, light

itself a lure. Lean into the patterned
motion, ripples to the north, standing waves

to the south, the steady shove—
toward what? Nothing here

is expected to make sense—contrary
intentions, even the charts

predict this. An improvisation
under the surface, revealed

by the interplay of light—
water with texture. Whatever invites attention

prayer enough for now. You could wait your whole
life for sense to take shape. Does it matter

from here, whether those are seals or
bull kelp? Keep looking.

MUSEUM PRAYER

You have left us alone long enough.
What fiasco did our obedience,
our silence, ever fend off?
Come back. Shed your disguises,
release yourselves from oil and frame, grace
open our mouths, walk again among—
press, pierce, consume—
us. Do again what we cannot.
Believe in us.

This Morning

Light takes the Tree; but who can tell us how?
—Theodore Roethke

It's time. It's almost too late.
Did you see the magnolia light its pink fires?
You could be your own, unknown self.
No one is keeping it from you.

The magnolia lights its pink fires,
daffodils shed papery sheaths.
No one is keeping you from it—
your church of window, pen, and morning.

Daffodils undress, shed papery sheaths—
gestures invisible to the eye.
In the church of window, pen, and morning,
what unfolds at frequencies we can't see?

Gestures invisible to naked eye,
the garden opens, an untranslatable book
written at a frequency we can't see.
Not a psalm, exactly, but a segue.

The garden opens, an untranslatable book.
You can be your own, unknown self—
not a psalm, but a segue.
It's time.

Not My Brother

he crosses the path of a blue sedan
bounces twice and embraces the road

his cheek pressed to asphalt
as if merely napping

sunlight splinters off the fractured windshield

a stranger   I run to him
frantic to see his chest rise or lips part

he is not my brother

if this is his last minute   here
in the middle of the road

let him be accompanied
give him   at least   a stranger's

touch   let him not be my brother
let him not   die alone

Winter Garden

nothing to be done
but wait   that's your whole job
resting and waiting and by god

that's difficult enough   giving up
everything you know
about resilience persistence
winning   listen

when the signal comes
and it always comes
we will all turn over
and begin again   facing the wind
and the place in the clouds
where we last felt sun

Dramatis Personae

My great, my grand, my mother: you know
what the dramatis personae demands.

To be the lead, you have to breed.
At best, a walk-on part, a cameo

for the maiden or childless aunt
bereft by misfortune (romantical)

or malfunction (anatomical).
You played the only parts conceivable.

What use, you fret, will the stars (the suitors,
the hoped-for-husband) have for me

uncastable anomaly? Let these
pages stand in for progeny, each line—

dear great, dear grand, dear mother mine—
the next link in the chain our labor made.

PHOTOGRAPH, 1990

Here's what I have: this picture. You, briefly home
from wherever you were becoming fluent next.

Blond hair, just beginning to thin, pulled back in a low ponytail. Worn
cotton turtleneck, jeans. The bespoke suits came later.

Nearly out of the frame already. A shoulder and most of an arm
uncontainable.

> Yes, I know. Any detail I offer leaves a skewed, incomplete view.
> Remember, it was Tom who wrote your eulogy. This
> is not your life story. Not mine, either.

I thought I saw you once in a tour guide's not-quite-perfectly timed jokes,
in his slightly archaic manners, the way he held the door.

He wore a royal blue cashmere muffler—remember, that one you lost
to the backseat of a London cab?

> I write "you" as if mere grammar could invoke you,
> as if my lack of memories were a problem
> we solve between us.

Your shadow dips over my newspaper as I read Krugman's column.
I want *your* explanation of what happened to the banks, the fate
   of the Euro.

> I'm trying to say what life is like without you in it—
> no, that's not quite right—

Some nights, I look out into the audience
and every face is yours.

MORE, ONE MORE

I claim I'll go still
full of curiosity.
But darling we both know
I always want one more
kiss, another drag
off the scent of your neck.
No reason to think I'll die
differently than I live—
hungry for one more mouthful
of honey, craving another blossom's
cargo of yellow, more
one more bass note
caressing my sternum, one more
saltwater swim.

I'm sure to try
to pull along some
cone or frond,
grain of sand
in my swimsuit, pistachio
stuck in my teeth—
to praise this world
by hauling what I can
into the next.
Darling, sweet pants,
don't stand
too close
at the end.

THE GIRL WHO GOES ALONE

Here's the thing about being a girl
and wanting to play outside.
All the grown-ups grind it into you from the get go:
girls outside aren't safe.
The guy in the car? If he rolls down the window and leans
        his head out, run
because the best you can hope for is a catcall, and at worst
you'll wind up with your face on the side of a milk carton.

Even when you're a grown-up girl, your father—because
        he loves you—
will send you a four-page article about how to protect yourself
while standing at the ATM, while travelling unescorted, while
        jogging solo
an article informing you how to distinguish phony police
and avoid purse snatchers, pickpockets, rapists, and thugs.

Tell someone you're going into the woods alone
and they'll story your head with trailside cougar attacks,
cave dwelling misogynists, lightning strikes, forest fires,
        flash floods,
and psychopaths with a sixth sense for a woman alone in a tent.

To be a girl alone in the wilderness is to know
that if something goes wrong—
you picked the trailhead where the ax murderer lurks
or the valley of girl-eating gophers—
if you don't come home intact, the mourning
will be mixed with I-told-you-sos
from everyone whose idea of camping involves an RV
        or a Motel 6.
The message is clear: Girls must be chaperoned.

So, when, at the end of the day, you zip up the tent
and lie back in your sleeping bag,
fleece jacket bundled into a lumpy pillow under your head,
the second you close your eyes every least night noise
    is instantly magnified.

You lie there and consider the pungent heft of menstrual blood,
how even your sweat is muskier, louder, when you're bleeding.
Not hard to imagine its animal allure—every bear
for miles around sniffing you on the night wind.

You lie there, listening, running a mental inventory of any
potentially scented item—
did every one make it into the food bag hung from a tree?
Toothpaste, trailmix, chapstick, sunscreen—fuck.
Sunscreen still in your pack, nestled right beside you
where Outdoor Man used to sleep. So you're up, out of the tent
headlamp casting its too-bright spotlight, darkening the dark
    outside its reach
as you lower the bag, shove the sunscreen in, hoist and tie.

Far enough from the ground to elude the bears?
Far enough along the branch to thwart raccoons?
Tree far enough from the tent to keep from signaling
the proximity of ground-level, girl-shaped snacks?

You go alone—in part—to prove that though Outdoor Man
    has left you
his body is the only geography he can deprive you of.
He can give his muscled calves and thighs, his shoulders, chest,
    and hands
to another woman, but not the Sauk River old growth,
snow fields of Rainier, sea stacks of Shi Shi.

He can keep you from the sweet, blood-thrilling hum
of his body, but not the sweaty, blood-thumping
pleasure of a hard-earned panoramic view or high altitude
   starlight.

The thing about being a girl who goes alone, who goes
again and again, is that it freaks
the potential next boyfriend. He doesn't want
to be out machoed and he doesn't want to admit it
and he hopes you can't tell. The thing
about being the girl who still goes alone is that it proves
you don't need him and no matter how you show him you
   want him
it's not the same
and you both know it.

Zipped back into the tent you remind yourself you've never
   really been in danger.
When have you ever been in danger? Well there was that boy
   but years ago
a teenager like you, driving around bored and pissed
at the world, his BB gun and his father's two rifles
on the seat beside him. Lucky you.
The gun he leveled on the window ledge
lodged nothing more than a BB in your thigh.

The thing about being a girl alone in the woods is
   you know too much
about the grain of truth in the warnings.

Even if you seem impervious, weird good luck leaving you
   so far unscathed
you know the other girls' stories—your sister
date raped after a party in college, a friend

raped by a stranger at knifepoint, the two women
shot on the Pinnacle Lake trail, the singer
killed by coyotes in Nova Scotia.

The thing
about being a girl
who goes alone
is that you feel like you shouldn't go
if you're afraid. If you go it should mean you're not afraid,
that you're never afraid. Your friends will think that you go
    unafraid.

This girl
who goes alone
is always afraid, always negotiating to keep the voices
in her head at a manageable pitch of hysteria.

I go knowing that there will be a moment—maybe
    long moments, maybe
hours of them, maybe the whole trip—
when I curse myself for going alone.
When I lie in the tent and all I am is fear.

I walk into the wilderness alone
because the animal in me needs to fill her nose
    with the scent of stone and lichen,
ocean salt and pine forest warming in early sun.

I walk in the wilderness alone so I can hear myself.
So I can feel real to myself.

I go because I know I'm lucky to have a car, gas money, days off
the back and legs and appetite

to take me there.
I go while I still can.

The girl who goes alone
claims for herself
the madrona   juniper   daybreak.

She claims hemlock   prairie falcon   nightfall
nurse log   sea star   glacial moraine
huckleberry   trillium   salal
snowmelt   avalanche lily   waterfall
birdsong   limestone   granite   moonlight   schist
cirque   saddle   summit   ocean
she claims the curve of the earth.

The girl who goes alone says with her body
the world is worth the risk.

SHI SHI BEACH

for Eric

Seagulls spread like a gray and white
beach towel abandoned

below the tide line.
My face hot with new sunburn

shoulders and hips buoyant
now the pack is set aside, the tent

assembled. My eyes rest
on the horizon, the seam

between ocean and air
unravels and shadows gather

in the forest at my back.
Shi Shi arcs northward, lets

the tide carry its pebbles
and the day's bootprints away.

You know I need this
like some people need

money or children or certainty—
to travel naked into an evening ocean

water rising with its own
irresistible rhythm, the chill

taking the soft place behind each knee,
crowning my hips as my fingers trail

in the slow current. I come here alone
to find with my feet

and whatever momentum I can gather
how deep we might go

how much
can be immersed and retrieved

and immersed.

Notes

"House Fire" is for Mik Kuhlman.

"The Permanent Fragility of Meaning." The title is taken from Jacques Attali's *Noise: The Political Economy of Music* (University of Minnesota Press, 1985).

"What Is Known." Michael Hobbs was a London School of Economics- and Yale-educated economist who was the first American lecturer at Masaryk University in the Czech Republic in the aftermath of the Velvet Revolution. He founded a successful stock brokerage with two of his former students and contributed to the development of laws regarding transparency in the emerging Czech capital markets. Because his partners had ousted him from the business some months earlier, his death in June 1997 was widely reported in the financial press and some speculated that he either had been murdered or had taken his own life. Though an autopsy ruled that he died naturally, it could not specify cause. He was 37.

"What We Would Forget." Prompted by Ellen Lauren's performance in the SITI Company's production of *Room*. The lines in italics are Virginia Woolf's words.

"Recompose." The phrase "a question mark, an unresolved ellipsis" is borrowed from Chris Abani's "Renewal," from *Sanctificum* (Copper Canyon Press, 2010).

"From Dr. Schnarch's Married People's Sex Manual." Every line is pilfered from the indispensable *Passionate Marriage: Keeping Love & Intimacy Alive in Committed Relationships* by David Schnarch, PhD (Henry Holt, 1997).

"Sarah" is for Sarah Gold Wallace, and for her mother, Anne.

"For You, First Through the Door" is for the police officers who found my brother's body in his Prague apartment. He had died five days earlier.

"Ebbing Hour" owes a debt to Stanley Kunitz's "The Long Boat."

"In Praise of Orality" is for Parker Johnson.

"Her, at Two" owes its beginning to Grace Rothmeyer, Sharon Olds, and Langston Hughes's poem "Luck."

"Where Currents Meet." Cattle Point, at the southwestern edge of San Juan Island in Washington State, is subject to strong currents where flows from the Haro Strait and the San Juan Channel mingle.

Acknowledgments

My gratitude to the editors of the following magazines and anthologies where these poems appeared, often in earlier versions:

Bellingham Review
Crab Creek Review
DMQ Review
The Moment Witnessed, Poems from Poets of the Fifth Skagit River Poetry Festival
Poets West
Pontoon: An Anthology of Washington State Poets
The Seattle Review
Switched-on-Gutenberg
Vox Populi
Willow Springs

In the Telling (eds. Susan Richardson and Gail Ashton, Cinnamon Press, 2009).

Jack Straw Writers (ed. Peter Pereira, Jack Straw Productions, 2003).

JumpStart: A Northwest Renaissance Anthology (Steel Toe Books, 2009).

Many Trails to the Summit (ed. David Horowitz, Rose Alley Press, 2010).

Poets Against the War (ed. Sam Hamill, Thunder's Mouth Press/ Nation Books, 2003).

Tattoos on Cedar (Washington Poets Association, 2006).

Vox Populi (ed. Catherine Martin, Eleventh Hour Productions, 2000).

Weathered Pages: The Poetry Pole (eds. Jim Bodeen, Terry Martin, Dan Peters, and Rob Prout, Blue Begonia Press, 2005).

Some of these poems also appeared in the chapbooks *The Girl Who Goes Alone* (Floating Bridge Press, 2010), produced with support from 4Culture/King County Lodging Tax Revenue, and *Where Currents Meet*, part of the quartet *Sightline* (Toadlily Press, 2010).

"Leaving the Island," "Problem Was," "The Girl Who Goes Alone," and "What Is Known" were commissioned for the 2009 Richard Hugo House Literary Series.

"On Punctuation" was featured on *The Writer's Almanac* on October 15, 2010, and printed as a beautiful limited-edition broadside by Joseph Green of The Peasandcues Press.

Appreciation

Depending on how you count it, I've been working on this book for ten years or my whole life. Either way, I'm grateful to many for help along the way:

To Chris Abani, Jane Hirshfield, and Nance Van Winckel for offering words and deeds of encouragement at crucial moments.

To Terry Martin for extending the initial invitations that led, ultimately, to this book's publication; Jim and Karen Bodeen, for planting the seeds and nurturing Blue Begonia into blossom; John Pierce for his sharp eye and deft copyeditor's touch.

To Dan and Amy Peters for their careful crafting of all the elements of this book. My deep gratitude to Dan for his insightful, patient editing as this manuscript found its final shape.

To 4Culture and the City of Seattle Office of Arts and Cultural Affairs for grants during the earliest stages of the writing process.

To Artsmith, Hedgebrook, the Helen Riaboff Whiteley Center, John Mellana and Suzanne Edison, and Erin Palmer for the gift of residencies that were vital to the development and completion of this collection.

To my colleagues at Seattle Children's Hospital, who make it possible for me to take the time away to write, especially Lisa Brihagen, Jennifer Fisch, and Jennifer Seymour. To Mark Power and the Children's staff and physicians who come to the monthly miniretreats, confirming my belief that poetry makes a difference in our daily lives.

To Megan Sukys, my producer at KUOW, whose questions over

the years have taught me so much about story, and about poetry.

To the Skagit River Poetry Festival, Jack Straw Writers
Program, and Richard Hugo House (especially Brian
McGuigan) for early, consistent encouragement.

To the faculty of Antioch University Los Angeles, especially
Frank X. Gaspar, Eloise Klein Healy and Ingrid Wendt, and
to all my classmates, particularly Hallie Moore, Peggy Hong,
Gayle Brandeis, and Valentina Gnup; to Leslie Ullman and my
workshop-mates in the Vermont College of Fine Arts post-
graduate program; and to Mark Doty and my fellow writers
in the Centrum chapbook workshop, for reading and critiquing
earlier versions of these poems.

To Tim Seibles, for reaching out in friendship, for hearing what
was possible before I did, and for saying so.

To Christine Deavel and John Marshall for the sustenance and
spark of their friendship.

To Mona Mansour, playwright with the soul of a poet. For
persevering.

To Susan Rich for imagining Booklift and inviting me in, and to
all Booklifters for their generosity, example, and smarts.

To Peter Pereira for making the suggestion, and Floating
Bridge Press for taking a chance on *The Girl Who Goes Alone.*
Myrna Goodman and Meredith Trede of Toadlily Press
for seeing *Where Currents Meet.* The shaping of those two
chapbooks directly influenced the making of this collection.

To fellow artists who help in ways too numerous to list,
sometimes without even knowing the difference they make:
Peter Aaron, Kelli Russell Agodon, Lana Hechtman Ayers,

Janna Cawrse Esarey, Kathleen Flenniken, Tess Gallagher, Gitana Girafalo, Sam Green, Nancy Guppy, Jana Harris, Paul Hunter, Jourdan Keith, Tim Kelly, Jared Leising, Marjorie Manwaring, Claudia Mauro, Brenda Miller, the late Jack Myers, Nancy Pearl, Sylvia Pollack, Midge Raymond, David Wagoner, and Robert Wrigley. (And you, the one whose name I am forgetting and will immediately recall with chagrin upon the publication of this book.)

To Melissa Gayle West, for recognizing and nursing the pilot light; Cathy Englehart, Heidi Gans, and Sharon Kaylen for wisdom and hands-on skill.

To Abby Enson, Cecelia Frye, Katy DeRosier, Heidi Turner, Carol Jenkins, Corina Lymburner-Green, Anne Wallace, Stephanie Hillman, Lilja Otto, Michelle Baker, Ruth Shure, and Kelly Johnson for the midwifery of true friendship.

To my sister Cathy, and my brothers Chris, Steven, and Tom, for all the ways you've supported me as an artist, and to our late brother, Michael, who would have been first in line to buy this book and to give me (spot-on) edits.

To my parents, for teaching compassion and generosity by example, and for seeing the writer in me before I did. I love you more than I can say.

And most of all, to Eric—Mr. Integrity, beloved instigator, first and fiercest reader. I choose you.

About the Author

Elizabeth Austen spent her teens and twenties working in the theatre and writing poems. A six-month solo walkabout in the Andes region of South America led her to focus exclusively on poetry. She earned a BFA in Theatre (acting) at Southern Methodist University and an MFA in Creative Writing (poetry) at Antioch University Los Angeles.

She is the author of two chapbooks, *The Girl Who Goes Alone* (Floating Bridge Press, 2010) and *Where Currents Meet* (one of four winners of the 2010 Toadlily Press chapbook award and part of the quartet *Sightline*). In 2006 she produced *skin prayers*, an audio CD of her poems.

Elizabeth produces poetry-related programming for KUOW 94.9, an NPR affiliate. Her interviews are available at kuow.org. She makes her living as a communications specialist at Seattle Children's Hospital, where she also offers retreats and journaling workshops for the staff.

Visit her online at elizabethausten.org.